SOVETICA

Caroline Clark lived for ten years in Moscow, where she met Andrei. They moved to Montreal for six years and now live in her hometown of Lewes. She works as a Russian translator and community interpreter. Her first collection is *Saying Yes in Russian* (Agenda Editions).

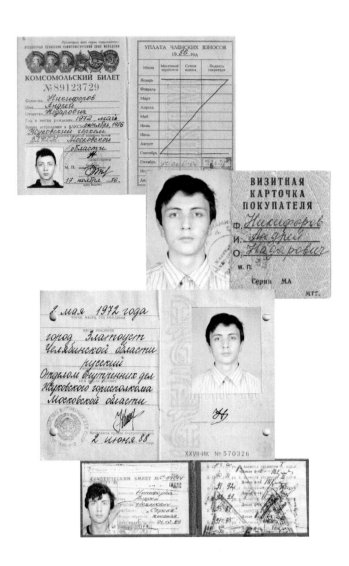

Никифоров Нодарович Андрей

Komsomol card
Rations card
USSR passport
Student card

SOVETICA

Caroline Clark

 editions

First published in 2021
by CB editions
146 Percy Road London W12 9QL
www.cbeditions.com

Printed in England by Imprint Digital, Exeter

ISBN 978–1–909585–43–0

For Greta and Christa

Acknowledgements

My thanks to Cōnfingō, *The Fortnightly Review* and *Tentacular*. I am especially grateful to Anthony Barnett, editor of *Snow lit rev*, who published the first extracts from this book.

My thanks to Kelda Folliard, Clare Hitchen, Alexandra Hudson and Ursula McGeoch for their early encouragement with the book.

My thanks to David Rose for his support and the afterword.

Finally, I thank the person whose stories these are: thank you, Andrei, for telling me your stories and letting me retell them. And thank you, Andrei and Ilya, for your slides and photographs.

Colour slides

By the snowplough (right side: Andrei, Yutsa, Oleg, Sliva)	front cover
By the pigeon loft (l to r: Pasha, Yutsa, Oleg, Sliva)	2
On the fence (Andrei and Pasha)	11
On the tracks (top: Oleg, Sliva, Yutsa, Pasha);	15
Railway depot (below: Sliva, Yutsa, Pasha, Oleg)	
In the stadium park (Pasha, Oleg, Sliva)	17
On the railings (Yutsa, Sliva, Pasha, Oleg)	21
Heavy metal graffiti (Yutsa and Sliva)	35
On the table frame (Sliva, Oleg, Yutsa, Pasha)	37
By the snowplough (left side: Andrei, Yutsa, Oleg, Sliva)	47
By the stadium (Sliva, Oleg, Pasha)	53

Black-and-white photos

Pasha and Vovchik (top); Andrei (below)	7
Dimon air guitar (top); Dimon and 'MacDosha' (below)	8
Andrei looking back	28
Dimon and Olga	30
Andrei stamping	32
Seryoga	41
Andrei in practice trenches (above); Stone grenade (below)	51

Contents

Scrapheap	1	Dragon	29
Town	3	Sweet	30
Broad	3	Flower	31
Chebureki	4	Pizzeria	33
Idiots	4	MacDonalds	33
Nose	5	Autograph	34
Pasha	6	Americans	36
Palich	9	Kiosk	37
Adventure	9	Job	38
Olympics	10	Documents	39
Boots	11	Homebrew	40
Grandmother	12	Cabbage	40
Duck	13	Rifle	41
Stars	13	Armchair	42
Elecktrichka	14	Letter	43
Bread	16	Factory	44
Hole	17	Overcoat	45
Lassie	18	Clothes	45
English	18	Book	46
Radio	19	Record	46
Baltics	19	Help	48
Free	20	Chalk	48
Joke	21	Culture	49
Bun	22	News	50
Ads	23	Spear	50
Ticket	24	Hammer	52
Soap	25	Field	53
Paste	25		
Haircut	26	Afterword by David Rose	54
Portrait	27	Note on the photographs	55

Scrapheap

The scrapheap was the
place we'd always go.
The centre of our lives.
Every yard had their
own one. You couldn't
just go to someone else's.
It was part of our yard.
There were sometimes
fights but usually we just
dredged through looking
for stuff.
                    Once
me and a friend found a
bottle with some white
liquid in it like milk. The
first thing he did of course
was to smash it against
the fence, but it flew past
the fence to where there
was a park we called the
little forest where people
used to beat their rugs.
A moment later an angry
woman came running
towards us covered in
white liquid. She tried
to grab my friend by his
ear, but he got away.

Town

For a long time I
thought the town
where I was born
was called Zlatoust.
When filling out
forms I would write
the town of Zlatoust.
Then one day my
mum told me that
it was in fact called
Zlatoust-36 or 33.
It was some kind
of classified town
with a name and
number that was
        on no maps.

Broad

Broadway was the main street.
Everyone's town had their own
broadway. That's what we all
called it. The widest longest
street. When we got together
we'd say let's go to the *broad*.

Chebureki

We had a lot of
stories about them.
Two friends. Ginger
bought a chebureki.
Horse asked if he
could have a bite.
Ginger said go on
and Horse bit the
middle out taking
all the meat. Ginger
was left with just
      the pastry.

Idiots

It was an exam
or test and they
were talking to
the teacher about
something, maybe
they were being
tested, and he said,
You're not fools,
you're idiots. Well,
they graduated
fine.
        Ginger
was a chess player
– very talented and
and he even got to
skip a year because
he was so clever.
Then he started
drinking and taking
drugs. He lost himself.
Horse was fine.
He was even quite
a good boxer. He
was always alone.
He was interesting,
always in his own
world. He has a job
      somewhere.

Nose

Ilya once broke my nose
when we were boxing. It
looked funny, crooked, to
one side. When I went to
school the next day the
whole class laughed and
the teacher said, Now you
look like a Georgian. So
I went to the doctors.
They took an x-ray and
said nothing was broken.
So we went to Moscow.
They took an x-ray and
said nothing was broken.
Then my dad took me to
a special forces hospital
where a huge surgeon
looked at me and said,
There's nothing on the x-
ray. So dad said, His nose
is crooked. Well, said the
surgeon, if it's crooked,
let's straighten it. And he
put it back in place with
his hands. Crunch and it
was done. He showed me
a mirror and asked, Is it
straight now? Not quite,
I said. So he crunched it
again. Then he asked my
dad, Is it ok now? It's ok
          now, he said.

Pasha

Pasha was very small
and fast. There were
three of them, brothers.
I used to mix them up
because they had the
same surname and
looked alike but Pasha
was the smallest. He
was quite a hooligan.
        We once got to
school, early morning,
and the whole corridor
was thick with smoke,
and in the smoke was
the headteacher. Later
on we discovered that
Pasha had got there
early – not to study –
but the day before he
had made a smoke
bomb and now he'd
let it off in the toilets.
There was so much
smoke that it filled
the toilets and corridor.
We knew it was Pasha
but didn't tell anyone.
He always did his own
thing. Always came up
with stuff to do. Always
ready for an adventure
but he looked very quiet.

Palich

There was a guy — Palich
I don't even remember his
real name. Everyone called
him Palich. Everyone loved
him. He wrote crazy poems
and then sang them with his
guitar although he couldn't
play the guitar.
        He strummed very
loudly and sang through his
nose. Everyone liked them
because something funny
always happened. He was
just a bit different. We would
have to talk him into it. And
when he said yes, we'd have
to quickly run for a guitar
before he changed his mind.
        I remember rushing
to Vovich's for his guitar
and we all sat at the stadium
with Palich singing complete
nonsense. I'm a country boy,
a country boy I am, come
visit me in the country and
I'll kick your balls right in.

Adventure

When America started bombing
Yugoslavia there were lots of pro-
tests. Palich went to Moscow. He
took an inkwell and threw it at
the American Embassy and got
arrested. He told us about it as
though it were a great adventure.

Olympics

When I started school in '79
the year before the Olympics
came to Moscow they told us
there'd be a lot of foreigners
and under no circumstances
to take any presents or sweets
from anyone. Some women
came and told us what to do.
       And once a man came
up to me outside when I was
with mum on the way to the
metro. He offered me a toy
tank and I really wanted it. I
took it but mum told me not
to as it might explode. I was
scared and left it by the metro.
And when I came back it was
                    gone.

Boots

We went to Lenin's
mausoleum and one
boy (last name Morozov
– we called him Moroz)
was wearing dirty boots
and the teacher said, How
dare you come to see Lenin
in dirty shoes. She brought
him up in front of everyone
and scolded him till he cried.
I wished my shoes were dirty
too as he got sent home.

Grandmother

She said, Don't forget
to pray to your darling
Lord. She called him
that like a baby. Pray to
him at bedtime, thank
him, think of him. My
mother's mother. I once
secretly made the sign of
the cross on my pillow
when I was at her place.
       But at school
our teacher told us very
sternly there was no God.
And if someone in your
family tells you otherwise
then ask them when and
how he ever helped them.
My mum told me how
when my grandmother
was ill she prayed and
got better. My dad never
went into a church because
you weren't supposed to.

Duck

My friend's mum was
given a duck to cook.
A drake, with a green
head. And in the end
they did cook it. But
it stayed with them in
the kitchen a while. I
went to see it. It was
there a few days and
then they cooked it.
But I don't think my
friend felt like eating
it. He took a piece
and threw it back.
Never one to complain.
But he did feel sorry
          for that duck.

Stars

When I was still at school
I really wanted a badge of
the American flag. And a
friend of mine said he had
one that even had stars on it,
a good one. He promised to
give it to me but never did.
He probably never even had
one. But I did get one from
an American exhibition,
          one with stars.

Elektrichka

There was a point where
the track forked off in a
direction I'd never been.
I wanted to see where it
went. And whenever I
passed this place I always
tried to see further up the
track. One day I decided
enough was enough and
I just got on the elektrichka
and rode there. I went a
little way then I walked
          back to my stop.

Bread

During the school holidays
there was a rhythm to the
day. In the morning we'd
go out to play then someone
would say, The film's starting
in five minutes, and we'd all
go in to our own or someone
else's home. The streets would
be deserted for a while and
when the film was over we'd
all go back outside.
          In the winter
there was Captain Vrungel,
The Life and Adventure of
Four Friends – about dogs,
and Guest From the Future.
In the summer they always
showed one about a boy
called Denis Korablyov and
The Adventures of Elektronik.
          Mum used to
leave food for me in a flask
and then later on she showed
me how to use the oven. But
sometimes I'd just come in,
take a piece of black bread,
sprinkle it with sugar then
          go back out.

Hole

Whenever I went to my
English tutor's house it
was very important that
I was clean and smartly
dressed. One day my mum
asked me whether I'd changed
my socks and I said yes I had
but I hadn't. I'd been playing
outside all day. When I got
to my tutor's house and took
my shoes off one sock had
a huge hole in it. My mum
went bright red and the tutor
said, No matter, no matter.

Lassie

I first watched Lassie
when I was very small.
It was just about a dog
so they showed it. But
we saw America. How
beautiful it was. For
some reason they let
us see everything we
                didn't have.

English

There was a channel
that showed language
programmes. One was
in English about foreign
children living with an
English family. There
was a Finnish boy who
used to like to eat a lot
and he always seemed
a little shy about asking
for more. The father would
try to encourage him saying,
Maybe a sausage? And
a voice from behind the
screen would say, Mikko
likes a big breakfast.

Radio

For breakfast we had
buckwheat porridge
(I hated it with milk)
or oat porridge called
Hercules. Dad would
get up first and turn
the radio on very loud.
He always had it on –
it was obligatory and
it used to be forbidden
to turn it off. We always
had fresh bread which
only lasted two days.
There were programmes
about what to do with
it when it turned stale.
School started at 8 a.m.
Shops opened at 8.30.

Baltics

Sherlock Holmes
was shot in the '80s
in the Baltic States.
It looked very foreign.
They always used
the Baltics for films
set abroad. Anything
from the West like
Prince Florizel and
James Chase.
        There were
also good Westerns
made in Yugoslavia.
The Indians were
always good and
the cowboys bad,
drunk and greedy.

Free

The whole idea was
to buy something for
free as we used to say.
Sometimes we'd say we
were testing communism
because everything was
supposed to be free.
       My mum once
sent me to buy bread and
vegetables and I asked my
friend to buy the bread as
it was in a different building.
When he came back with
the bread he also gave me
back the money and said
he'd bought it for free.

Joke

During perestroika
the school principle
told us a joke. He
was a party member
but had a good sense
of humour.

    A son asks
his father, Father is
Brezhnev good? His
father replies, We'll
find out soon enough
    when he dies.

Bun

I once went into a shop
and saw a friend begging
for money to buy a bun.
I just took one, put it in
my pocket and left. But
I took it out of my pocket
too soon when the shop-
keeper was looking out
the window. She came
running after me and I
ran. There were people
at the bus stop and a
man held me while the
shopkeeper took my bag
off me – I was on my way
home with my sports kit
– and she said she'd only
give it back if I brought
my mother with me.

For a few days I
lied and made up stories
about why I didn't have
my bag. Once when we
passed the shop just by
chance my sister asked
to go in and buy some-
thing but I said let's just
go home. I didn't want
us to go in. But in the
end my mum found out
somehow. When she took
me to the shop I realised
that she knew everything.

Ads

When there was very
little food in the shops
and all the shelves were
bare and people were
poor — at that time we
had what they called
telebridges with America
and they used to show
adverts between the talking.
They showed them for
the Americans but we
also got to see them for
some reason. They were
even translated.

        One ad was
for a Chrysler. Chrysler —
the keys to your happiness.
And another was for a Sony
TV. It was as if they were
from another world. In
America you could just
go and buy a Sony TV —
a beautiful TV so bright
with all the colours of the
rainbow — Trinitron. We
had a black-and-white
TV so I couldn't see all
the colours of the rainbow.

Ticket

Lemonade was expensive.
It cost 50 to 60 kopeks.
Bread was 16 kopeks for
black and white was 20.
For school mum gave me
20 kopeks so I could buy
a glass of juice for 10 and
bread with a thick slice of
kolbasa for the other 10.

          But I
often lost my money and
I would go without lunch
because we used to play
heads or tails for money.
Kvas was 3 kopeks for a
small mug, 6 for medium
and 8 large. Clothes were
expensive. Jeans were 100
rubles. Mum earned about
200 rubles a month and
dad about 300. Mum paid
30 rubles a month for me
to go to art school. Tutors
were expensive.

          A taxi was 1 ruble
in town. A train ticket was
about 50 kopeks to Moscow.
The bus about 5 kopeks. You
could travel for less if when
you gave the money to the
woman you said, No need
for a ticket. She'd take the
money and you'd give less
than it actually cost. Someone taught me and I used
to do that. It was okay to
steal from the government
but not from a person.

Soap

There was domestic soap.
Dark brown. They said it
was made from stray dogs.
We used it for washing our
clothes. We had a washing
machine but it didn't work.
It was Soviet. We used it
the once then it flooded
the people below and we
stopped using it. We put
our clothes into the bath-
tub, filled it up with water
and a little soap, lathered
them up and scrubbed the
clothes on a board, then
rinsed them out. For our
hair we used any soap. I
used one called Children's
Soap. I'd lather myself all
over including my head.

For the dishes we
had a greasy cloth which
soaked up all the grease
and we just washed the
dishes with lots of water.
Sometimes with boiling
water from the kettle.

Paste

There were two or three types
of toothpaste. Forest Paste was
bright green and had a medicinal
smell. Children's Paste was sweet
– and we sometimes tried eating
it at summer camp. And then there
was tooth powder. One type was
called Special Powder. It smelled
nice and made your teeth squeak.

Haircut

At the hairdresser's there
were only two or three
haircuts to choose from.
Close-shaved for 40 kop-
ecks. With the Youth cut
they'd leave you a bit of
hair. I always had the 40-
kopeck cut – very short –
and I hated it so I always
tried to get out of going
there. The teachers would
sometimes make me go.
I'd watch as my hair would
fall to the ground leaving
me pretty much bald.
                    Only
once when I asked them
to take off just a little did
they leave me with a lot
and I was happy. Then for
1 ruble 30 there was an
elite style called Model's
haircut. I had it done once
when I was older. They left
me with a strange quiff. The
Contemporary was like a
fascist's haircut – with a
long fringe at the front.

Portrait

First of all Brezhnev
died and there was
sad music on the TV.
They cancelled all the
programmes and only
left us the bedtime story.
But the main thing was
that school closed for
the day of his funeral.
Only the straight-A kids
were unhappy as they
had to stand in front of
his portrait all day.
            Then
came Andropov and just
over a year later he died.
We were so happy as we
thought there would be
no school. And there really
was no school except for
the straight-A kids again
who had to stand in front
of his portrait.
            Then
came Chernenko who was
called the living corpse as
he was on so much med-
ication, very old, just like
a living mummy. A year
later he died and we were
all happy but it turned out
that school wouldn't be
closing for his funeral. We
all said how disrespectful.

Dragon

In every Soviet school
there was a bust of Lenin
made out of cheap plaster
and hollow inside. And
every Soviet schoolchild
knew more or less how to
make a smoke bomb using
saltpeter cigarette paper.
    I once heard
of someone using a nail
to make holes in Lenin's
nostrils and then putting
a smoke bomb inside.
Very soon smoke started
coming out of his nostrils
like a zmei gorynych.

Sweet

In school the idea
was that when it
came everything
would be free.
Someone would
offer me a sweet
and say, You can
have it for free
when communism
comes but for now
you can buy it.
When we were
very small we'd
steal things and
say we'd comm-
unismed them.

Flower

The 7th of November
always fell during our
autumn break and on
that day we always had
to march in the parade.
It took up half a day at
least. Worst of all was
when they made you
carry a banner because
they'd always make you
haul it back to school
afterwards. If you were
only carrying a balloon
you could just pop it
after. We'd always try
to get one as you had
to carry something.
Before it started we'd
fill our pockets with
bits of broken glass
to throw at the girls'
balloons. Once a
friend of mine was
given a big fake flower
on a stick to carry. He
stuck a nail into the
end of it.

Our school
was the worst in town
so we always had to
march last and let the
other schools go ahead.
Worst of all was when
the bigger boys used
to make us haul their
banners back to school.
Later when
I joined a sports school
we marched first ahead
of all the schools. They
gave me a certificate
so my school wouldn't
make me do it as well.
We wore our kimonos
and were allowed to
carry nothing at all.

Pizzeria

When it opened
we were told not
to go there unless
we wanted to get
             poisoned.

                    MacDonalds

                    When it opened it was
                    all really expensive and
                    there was always a huge
                    queue so we jumped it a
                    few times and got in but
                    all I could afford was a
                    hamburger. Then one day
                    I bought a Big Mac and
                    decided to take it home
                    and divide it into four so
                    everyone could try a bit.
                    It was tasty. We liked it.
                    But one day a friend of
                    mine who used to work
                    out a lot ate one and was
                    ill. He suspected that it
                    wasn't so good after all.

Autograph

I first got into them
because of the album
covers. Then a friend
from art school lent me
a recording and before
I'd even listened to it I
knew I'd like it. I was
very lucky when they
came to Moscow as I
managed to get into
their dressing rooms
posing as an interpreter.
Someone had promised
to meet me and get me
into the concert but no
one turned up and there
was an Englishman running
around shouting, Where's
the interpreter – and I said
it was me. No one knew
anyone else, people who
were supposed to know
said, Yes, yes, that's him
and everyone was relieved.
They put some tags on me
and told me to go into the
dressing rooms and not
let anyone one in. It
was like a dream when
suddenly I saw some
band members and I
asked the manager if I
could get an autograph.
I was told no. I hardly
understood anything
they said, so I just nodded.

As soon as I saw
Steve Harris I asked him
for an autograph and an
Englishman ripped off my
tags and chased me out
shouting. Security came
up to me and said I'd
caused them a lot of
trouble and asked who
I was. I felt awkward
but on the other hand
I didn't give a damn.

Later I styled my
signature on Steve Harris's.
It's not exactly the same
but similar. And when I
worked in a bank part
of my job was to sign
off loans on forms and
I used this signature. I
still do.

Americans

Firmà was what we
called foreigners. We'd
call out, The firmà are
here, or Look they've
brought the firmà. A
man was firmach and
a woman firmachka.
                    Their
things always had a
special smell. And
when they walked
past or when we
opened a new t-shirt
we'd just exchanged
we'd say it smells of
firmà. Most fragrant
of all were Americans.

Kiosk

When I used to go home
from the Library of Foreign
Literature, I'd take the number
45 and at Novaya station there
was a kiosk where I'd buy a box
of crackers and a litre of beer
for the train ride home.

Job

My father was in the army
and he decided that it was
time for me to get a job –
I had long hair – and my
first boss was a friend of
my father's. On the first
day he told me to get a
haircut. I came in on the
second day with only the
front cut. He told me to
turn about face – in the
military style – following
which there was a shout
and he reprimanded me
for not cutting the back.
It was the kind of job you
couldn't get. Classified.
I was to stand there and
open and close the door.
Policemen worked along-
side me. One day a cashier
rushed up to us horrified.
She had been sitting there
wondering why there were
no customers. It turned out
a cop had locked the door
so he could sit down and
                      read.

Documents

When I was a security
guard there was a talk
by criminologists and
they told us how doc-
uments were falsified.
The type that used to
be written in black ink
with no plastic covering.
　　　　　They would
take a thin-tipped pen
filled with a sweet syrup
and very carefully trace
over the text with a thin
layer of this sweet syrup
and then they'd put the
documents in a box with
black cockroaches who
would gnaw away at the
sugar along with the ink
– they have very sharp
teeth – and they'd take
off a thin layer of paper,
so thin you couldn't see,
and the document would
become a blank. And you
could write whatever you
　　　　　　　　wanted.
Which is what they did.

Homebrew

Yura had some and
I said I'd have a little
as long as there was
something to wash it
down with. They gave
me a small glass of it
and a big glass of juice.
I drank it, then started
on the big glass but I
couldn't understand
why it was burning my
throat so much. They
had given me a small
glass of the strong stuff
followed by a big one.

Cabbage

When we were students
one guy said he didn't
want to drink anymore
and they said, Well will
you have something to
eat, he said, I will but
not drink, and they said,
Will you have pickled
cabbage, he said, I will,
so they took a glass of
vodka and mixed it in
with the cabbage and he
he ate it all. Then he said,
I think the cabbage is off.

Rifle

Once we were drinking
with two policemen.
Neither of them could
stand and suddenly
their radio called and
one of them tried so
hard to pull himself
together and take the
call. They were good
guys. I think I might
have got to hold a rifle.

Armchair

One summer I worked on
a building site. We used to
sit around till about 11 doing
nothing because there was no
cement. It was usually 12.30
by the time they brought the
cement and lifted it up to us
on a crane at which time we'd
all go home for lunch. When
we came back the cement had
always dried out and we would
be unable to use it so we would
have to wait for the next batch.
Sometimes they would bring it
just before the end of the day,
sometimes it would come straight
away and we would have to start
work. But we never worked in
the mornings as there was never
any cement. We didn't work in
the rain either.
                One morning
because it was boring doing
nothing I got hold of all the
bricks lying around and built
myself an armchair and so
did my other two friends. We
made 3 armchairs, like sun
loungers, out of bricks and
we lay back and sunbathed.
It was a beautiful August.

Letter

My friend and I were working on
a building site where we were
supposed to put bricks inside the
walls but no one put bricks inside
the walls because all the bricks had
been stolen so they put rubbish in
there instead. We found an empty
bottle and decided to write a letter
to whoever would find it, full of
swear words. Then we put it
in the wall and closed it up.

Factory

I had the chance to work
in a factory for a month.
They told everyone to
bring a black work coat.
I didn't look for one and
forgot about it but the
day before work started
I remembered and asked
my mum. She didn't have
a black one but she had a
white one as she was an
engineer. A white one
like doctors have. I took
it and went to work. After
about two days I realised
that everyone thought I
was an engineer or boss
so I stopped working and
just walked around the
factory floor. No one
questioned me. I walked
around talking to people
and they spoke politely
to me. One time I saw
a women about to steal
something. She saw me
and was scared. I said,
Don't worry I didn't see
                    anything.

Overcoat

When I went to work
on the Arbat I started
selling army uniforms
including my father's.
There was his overcoat
in the wardrobe which
I sold for 20 or 30
dollars – two months
of my mother's wages.
At that time my dad
was still in the army
and one day he needed
to go to Moscow to the
headquarters. When he
went to get his coat
from the wardrobe it
simply wasn't there.

Clothes

Mum used to buy clothes
from street sellers. Everyone
knew where to find them.
You had take the elektrichka
to another stop. There were
also some sellers that stood
outside shops. She liked to
look for things that had been
made in Yugoslavia. She once
took my dad but they could
tell from the way he walked
that he was a military man
and thought he was from the
police so she stopped going
with him and took me instead.

Book

During perestroika I once
saw a priest selling bibles.
He had one copy of the
New Testament left. Very
slim printed on American
paper. I asked him to put
it to one side for me as I
didn't have any money on
me. I said I'd go and get
some and come back. I
ran as I was worried that
someone else would buy
it. But when I came back
the book was still there.
He said, Read it, read it.

Record

I heard a guy singing
bicycle, bicycle. I just
liked the way he sang
it and asked who's that?
Then I went to the record
shop and bought it there.

Help

There was a long queue
when they came to town
with the watermelons.
You had to stand in line
for almost the whole day.
The whole neighbourhood
was there, everyone knew
everyone else. Parents and
children. I offered to help
the seller and hand her the
watermelons. When it was
our turn I handed her the
best ones.

Chalk

One day someone
told me you could
eat chalk so I tried.
Later when I was at
an English lesson with
a private tutor she had
to go out for a minute.
When she came back
she looked puzzled
wondering where
the chalk had gone.

Culture

We went by train to Georgia
the year before the war started.
At that time in Russia all the shops
were empty and there was nothing
left to drink. All the eau de cologne
had been drunk, all the lotions. And
when we got to Georgia I saw that
not only was there eau de cologne
in stock but there was even vodka.
People had their own homes in the
mountains with verandas. They had
cars. And culture too. Little children
played make-believe, the older ones
played billiards. Where we came from
little children just rooted through the
rubbish heaps, the big ones too.

News

On the night Yeltsin
came to power we
were all watching TV
and the newsreader
said, Goodnight every-
body, be free. It was
as if we had been
given our freedom.

Spear

One time when there were elections
and all the candidates were communists
and there were glass framed posters of
them everywhere me and a friend found
a huge stick which became a spear and
we were knights and shouted charge and
hit the glass. We smashed one frame first
and had so much fun that we went along
the street – it was very long – smashing as
many as we could until it was time to go
to school. Later on we smashed the rest.

Hammer

For two days I worked at
a conveyor belt. Everyone
there was given a big heavy
wrench or hammer. I asked
what it was for and they said
if you can't keep up with the
speed or if something breaks
you should bash one of the
metal tracks and everything
will stop and someone will
come and fix it. I soon got
tired so I broke part of the
belt and everything stopped
                    for good.

Field

Me and Sliva once rode
a bike across the big field.
Pasha was there too. Sliva
pedalled and I just sat on
the bag rack. We set out
into the wide field and the
sun was setting. It was July.
Warm. And there was this
                    light.

Afterword by DAVID ROSE

In a time of increasingly sterile autofiction, this project comes to me as a breath of fresh air – air from another time, another place; the texts gritty, resolutely non-literary, each ending with a narrative shrug.

When I read an early batch of these texts, I responded instantly to that matter-of-fact authenticity, because, I realised later, of their resonance with my own childhood and adolescent memories, the resemblance between late-communist Russia and post-war Britain.

I was born in 1949; my childhood spanned the Fifties. I had my own ration book – sweets, along with other things, were rationed until the mid-Fifties. There were few washing machines; laundry was done by hand, with blocks of laundry soap, then put through a hand mangle, then onto the line. You could buy, well into the Sixties, sachets of shampoo from Woolworth's, enough for a single hair wash, although we made them do for two. Toilet paper was Izal, which had the texture of tracing paper and the scent of disinfectant.

We lived in Egham, a rural district council; houses, at least council houses, all had 'pig bins', in which scraps of food and peelings were saved and collected by the council for use by local pig farmers. In my teens, a Wimpyburger, or a frothy coffee (they weren't called cappuccinos then) in Kardomah, was the height of sophistication.

So my response was at once personal, nostalgic, and literary – or maybe anti-literary – to the authenticity of this project, its deliberate short-circuiting of literary technique. Although, paradoxically, that authenticity is enhanced, or rather preserved, by the filters of its production.

Some years after first seeing these slides, Caroline started recording Andrei reminiscing in Russian about his childhood and teenage years. These stories were then translated into English by Caroline and, with the lightest revision, formatted into prosaic blocks of text. These blocks became *Sovetica* – painting a very raw, instantly nostalgic but intensely personal record of what is fast becoming a forgotten era. Poems? Stories? Defying category, they recreate this past – the grey gerontocracy of late communism – and in so doing, revitalise the literary present.

Note on the photographs

The colour photos are scanned images of 35mm slides made by Andrei Nikiforov, Caroline Clark's husband, over the course of a few days in 1989 in his hometown of Zhukovsky, 25 miles south-east of Moscow. That year Andrei had learnt how to make 3D – or stereo – slides from an article in the *Young Technician* magazine. He read how the photographer should take two exposures on positive film, with slightly different camera positions. The method was simple: rock onto one leg to take the first shot and then over onto the other leg to take the second shot; the subjects must hold their pose through-out both shots. When developed the slides would then be viewed through a stereo slide viewer (below)to give a 3D effect. The film was expensive and occasionally on sale in Zhukovsky. It was made by the East German company Orwo Chrom and could only be devel-oped at one shop on Kalininsky Prospect in Moscow.

The slides have now been digitally converted but retain their low-tech aura. Being transparencies there is one quality that cannot be conveyed on the pages here: the light. To view them one must look into the light – towards a window or lamp – and it is this that brings them to life. The images acquire depth, with every leaf and puddle and scrap of rubbish sharply distinct.

The black-and-white photos were taken by Andrei's best friend, Ilya. They show some of the same boys, including Andrei.

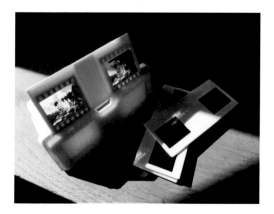

Ⓑ *editions*

Founded in 2007, CB editions publishes chiefly short
fiction and poetry, including work in translation.
Books can be ordered from www.cbeditions.com.